THE OVAL PORTRAIT
AND OTHER POEMS

The Oval Portrait
and other poems

by
KATHLEEN RAINE

THE ENITHARMON PRESS

HAMISH HAMILTON

1977

First published in 1977 by the Enitharmon Press
22 Huntingdon Road London N2 9DU
in association with Hamish Hamilton Limited
90 Great Russell Street London WC1

THE ENITHARMON PRESS
SBN 901111 96 1

HAMISH HAMILTON
SBN 241 89516 2

Acknowledgements are due to the Malahat Review,
Ariel (University of Calgary), Littack, New
Departures, the Southern Review and the Tablet,
where some of these poems first appeared.

*Printed and made in Great Britain by Skelton's Press
Cannon Place Wellingborough Northants*

CONTENTS

07205

MUSIC

Ah, beautiful intangible
Country we can set no foot upon,
Nor kiss that earth, nor lay body down on
To weep, or sleep, or lie in grave,
No, nor by footfall come home,
Travelling out of time on these Mozartian waves,
Whose heavy hearts beat base
To so high heavenly a treble and multiple concord.

AUTUMN

Leaf-fall,
And the longed-for missed again
Between the coming and the gone;
Yet in tree's thinning leaves the crown
In this faded year-worn scrawl,
Blade's blot, bare stroke of petiole
Wind-tattered on a ragged sky
Stands ciphered still.

DREAM

How did I come, last night,
To that great mansion of the dead,
Night-house whose empty rooms were dense with fear?
Why did I dread their presences, who had been dear,
My heart throb with terror
Lest I see faces not human
That once shone on me with familiar love?

SECRET COMPANION . . . . .

Secret companion
Whose face I have never seen,
Absent these many years,
Have you been sad, as I, that we no longer
As once, wander bright fields together?
Do daimons mourn to see
Earthly charges stray away
Into blind mists and shadowy cities,
Lost on strange roads of time, détours, blind turnings?
Have you, invisible one,
Learned from my life-long story the sad wisdom
Of earth, and stilled the song
That once I heard at heart?
Or will you, on a dream's frontier,
Return and speak to me some morning,
And let us comfort one another?
Tell me again of spirit's undying joy,
And I will tell how we who walk the world
In merciful forgetfulness traverse
Moment by moment, little by little, this great plane of sorrow.

NOVEMBER DREAM

I wake to sycamore's yellowing leaves against the gray
Of cloud and London brick,
Day's solid walls and faintly luminous sky;
And still I almost see, in mind's eye,
Last night's woodland way
I followed under boughs of gold
Bathed in another light than these
That stand outside my window's narrow space.
No separation set me there, as here, apart
From dream's afresh-created sky and trees.
In that remembered country I was there indeed
While here, in body locked away,
Touch solid wood, wet leaves, earth-coloured flowers
And all is other that I feel and see;
Yet this world we call real, that has no place.

WHAT IS IT TO BE OLD . . . . .

What is it to be old
But to dwell in far places
Among young faces,
Young voices and laughter,
Young prowess and pride of feature
In the remembered gardens, the familiar houses
Of the dead.

ACACIA TREE

Day by day the acacia tree
With gold of noon and evening sun
Through airy quivering leaves made play
In shadow underleaf, and gay

Mirrors tossing blades of light
Various before your failing sight.
Four pigeons plumed in rose and gray
Browsed spring buds of the tree's crown
And heavy white and fragrant flowers
To petal-fall in summer hung
Until mid-August's dulling leaves
Began to cast their yellow coin.

As time for you ran swift away
Moment by moment, day to night,
Nature's illuminated book,
No two moving hours the same,
Lay always open at one page
Where Tree in its long present stood,
September day by golden day.
Only before eyes new-born,
Eyes fading, does the mystery stay,
A presence neither come nor gone.

THE OVAL PORTRAIT: JESSIE WILKIE, 1880-1973

At eighteen, you stood for this faded photograph,
Your young hand awkwardly holding the long skirt
Over that light foot no trammelling at your heels could stay,
The constricting blouse framing in the eighteen-nineties
The young girl whose round sweet face,
Soft shining curls piled above fine brows and wild-bird's eyes
Has such a proud air of freedom and happy heart.

You were in love, that day,
Only with the beautiful world, that lay,
You thought, in your life's untold story,
As you, fledged for womanhood, ready to soar,
Stood poised before the camera's dark glass
Untouched by the shadow sorrow casts before
On all such inviolate light-heartedness.

Those young eyes, unfaded by your ninety years
Still saw in each day earth's wonders new-begun,
Each yesterday a leaf sinking into a dark pool
Of a swift sky-reflecting burn.
All for you was always the first time, or the last,
Every parting for evermore, but free each happy return
Of memory's unforgiveness, memory's remorse.

Your spirit fast in time's jesses, still you turned
On death's camera obscura that proud look,
Expectant, though not unafraid; after his first stroke
'I was interested', you said; as the goshawk,
Its hood lifted then drawn down again
Over the golden eyes, is restless to go free
On unencumbered wings home to its wilderness.

16

CARD-TABLE

Always you were ready, revived by a good cup of tea,
To open the leaves of the folding table into a world
And from your rosewood box inlaid with ivory
Brought out the cards, the markers, or the board,
Switched off the flicker of the television screen
Where blacks and whites merge into indifferent grey
For an emblematic country where you, its queen,
Moved pawns and kings in errantry
Of ebony Spenserian knights and horses trapped in gold
Whose sovereigns held in check imperious heart and sword
And the invisible reaper delved his single spade
For lords of castle perilous and dark tower,
Your pitched court, your ever-embattled realm.

You liked to win; I too, though with less passion
Than you whose real world was all imagination
Untarnished by those ninety years that dimmed your sight and
                                            locked your fingers
While you and I wore out whole packs and sets of great ones
As tide of fortune ebbed and flowed, or skill prevailed
For you, by luck or extra-sensory perception favoured,
(Familiarly by your Scottish theologians named Old Nick.)
But no sermons could restrain those wild ancestors of yours
From poetry, whisky, games of chance with cards or dams
Or their own brave blood-gilt persons ventured on the field
With no reprieve, honour and pride at stake
And hearts to mourn when knaves prevailed.
How well you would have played their reckless gamblers' game of life!
Now what a world of magic with that box is shut.

YOUR GIFT OF LIFE WAS IDLENESS

Your gift of life was idleness,
As you would set day's task aside
To marvel at an opening bud,
Quivering leaf, or spider's veil
On dewy grass in morning spread.
These were your wandering thoughts, that strayed
Across the ever-changing mind
Of airy sky and travelling cloud,
The harebell and the heather hill,
World without end, where you could lose
Memory, identity and name
And all that you beheld, became,
Insect wing and net of stars
Or silver-glistering wind-born seed
For ever drifting free from time.
What has unbounded life to do
With body's grave and body's womb,
Span of life and little room?

18

THE LEAF

"How beautifully it falls", you said,
As a leaf turned and twirled
On invisible wind upheld,
How airily to ground
Prolongs its flight.

You for a leaf-fall forgot
Old age, loneliness,
Body's weary frame,
Crippled hands, failing sense,
Unkind world and its pain.

What did that small leaf sign
To you, troth its gold
Plight 'twixt you and what unseen
Messenger to the heart
From a fair, simple land?

HER ROOM

At first, not breathed on,
Not a leaf or a flower knew you were gone,
Then, one by one,

The little things put away,
The glass tray
Of medicines empty,

The poems still loved
Long after sight failed
With other closed books shelved,

And from your cabinet
Remembrances to one and another friend
Who will forget

How the little owl, the rose-bowl,
The Brig-o'Doone paperweight,
The Japanese tea-set

Lived on their shelf, just here,
So long, and there,
Binding memories together,

Binding your love,
Husband and daughter in an old photograph,
Your woven texture of life

A torn cobweb dusted down,
Swept from the silent room
That was home.

WITH A WAVE OF HER OLD HAND

With a wave of her old hand
She put her past away,
Ninety years astray
In time's fading land,

With that dismissive gesture
Threw off pretence,
Rose to her proud stature,
Had done with world's ways,

Had done with words,
Closed her last written book
To ponder deeper themes
In unrecorded dreams.

GOLDEN BUILDERS, 1974
for Michael and Frances Horovitz

O lovely mild Jerusalem
Whose hope is like a memory,
Are you a city or a dream
Or in your always coming down
From heaven to earth, from thought to form
Transient as music in the air,
Where we may set no foot upon
Towers and arches built of sound,
Intangible as heart's desire?

Descending angels in a dream
Inspire the plan the dreamer lays
With square and compass on the floor,
But visions out of time and place
Returning, carry soon away;
Yet here or there the temple shines,
Its seven lamps with tongues of flame
Encircle and illuminate
Sanctuaries of exiled man.

In England's gray polluted land
Our cities are not walled with gold,
But ground-plan, sketch, or little phrase
Is there, one evening, in some house
Of friendship, music, or of books,
In cloister, garden, concert-hall
Some detail of the master-plan,
Tomorrow lost, is found today,
And memory is like a hope
As we repair, remake, build on.

STORM-STAYED

Holy, holy holy is the light of day
The gray cloud, the storm wind, the cold sea,
Holy, holy the snow in the mountain,
Holy the stone, the dry heather, the stunted tree,
Holy the heron and the hoodie, holy
The leaf and the rain,
The cold wind and the cold wave, cold light of day
And the turning of earth from night into morning,
Holy this place where I am,
The last house, it may be,
Before the wind, the shelterless sky, the unbounded sea.

FOR THE VISITOR'S BOOK

Canna House, 1975
For John and Margaret

The cards that brighten the New Year,
A Christmas-tree grown in the wood,
The crimson curtains drawn, the owl
Whose porcelain holds a lamp to read
The music on the Steinway grand
Piano with its slipping scores
Of Couperin, Chopin and Ravel —
John and Margaret Campbell made
This room to house the things they treasure,
Records of Scotland's speech and song,
Lore of butterfly and bird,
And velvet cats step soft among
Learned journals on the floor.

More formal state across the hall,
The silver of the house displayed,
And ivory ladies, Chinese birds
Surveyed by Romney's General
Sir Archibald, whose following eyes
Seem with cool justice to appraise
Guests of the house who come and go.
His scarlet, silver order, sword,
Give him the advantage as he stands
Relaxed, Imperial Madras
His pictured background, ours a world
That now breeds few he would approve,
That kindly but commanding man

Who played the part his rank assigned
And governed by a law deemed just
As Indian Arjuna before,
Taught by his god to act, though slain
And slayer were of equal worth.
The rule of duty had not changed
With other empire, other race,
Though oftener in our day ignored
By innovators, who to make
A new world would destroy old ways.

In Scotland it is Hogmanay
Most warms the feelings of the heart,
Religion older than the old,
The cycle of perpetual things
In years that pass and years to come.
Here children sing from memory
Ancestral island tunes that praise
Those best of loves that never change
Though new men bear their fathers' names,
Boatmen and herdsmen of these shores.
We feast on venison from a neighbouring hill
Under that Campbell general's eye,
The drone of pipes across the bay,
The pibroch, 'Cattle of Kintail'
Played by the piper of the isle.

MAIRE MACRAE'S SONG

The singer is old and has forgotten
Her girlhood's grief for the young soldier
Who sailed away across the ocean,
Love's brief joy and lonely sorrow:
The song is older than the singer.

The song is older than the singer
Shaped by the love and the long waiting
Of women dead and long forgotten
Who sang before remembered time
To teach the unbroken heart its sorrow.

The girl who waits for her young soldier
Learns from the cadence of a song
How deep her love, how long the waiting.
Sorrow is older than the heart,
Already old when love is young:
The song is older than the sorrow.

DESERTED VILLAGE ON MINGULAY

From a photograph by Margaret Fay Shaw Campbell

Not far had men's hands to raise from the stony ground
Blocks the ice and rain had hewn.
The dry-stone walls of the houses of Mingulay still stand
Long after the sheltering roof is gone.
Not far had the heather thatch to blow back to the moor.

Children were born here, women sang
Their songs in an ancient intricate mode
As they spun the wool of sheep on the hill
By a bog turf fire hot on the swept hearth-stone.
Earth's breast that nourished and warmed was near
As cow-byre and lazy-bed
Made fertile with sea-wrack carried up from the shore
In creels of withies cut in a little glen,
Near as shelter of hill-side, fragrance of clover-scented air.

Not far had the dead to go on their way of return,
Not far the circle of the old burial-ground
Whose low wall sets its bound to encroaching wild
That never has put on pride of human form,
Worn face of maiden or fisherman, mother or son.
Never far the washer of shrouds, the hag with gray hair;
Yet those who here lived close to the mother of all
Found, it may be, in her averted face, little enough to fear.

BINAH

Lifelong the way —
I never thought to reach her throne
In darkness hidden, starless night
Her never-lifted veil;
Too far from what I am
That source, sacred, secret from day;
But, suddenly weeping, remembered
Myself in her embrace,
In her embrace who was my own
Mother, my own mother, in whose womb
Human I became.
Not far, I found, but near and simple as life,
Loved in the beginning, beyond praise
Your mothering of me in flesh and blood.
Deep her night, but never strange
Who bore me out of the kind animal dark
Where safe I lay, heart to heartbeat, as myself
Your stream of life carrying me to the world.
Remote your being as the milky way,
Yet fragrance not of temple incense nor symbolic rose
Conforted me, but your own,
Whose soft breasts, nipples of earth, sustained me,
Mortal, in your everlasting arms.
Known to the unborn, to live is to forget
You, our all,
Whose unseen sorrowing face is a farewell,
Forgotten forgiver of forgetfulness.
Lifelong we seek that longed-for unremembered place.

NOT THAT I HAVE FORGOTTEN

Not that I have forgotten,
Not that those poignant days
From the long present of the world are gone,
But that I no more choose to open
My book of life to scan
The record of lost years until the last is written.
Then, being freed from time, as the dead are,
I will be again
Where every tide-wet shell, each intricate ripple of the running burn,
Scent of birch in the first thaw of spring, remain;
To the very place and hour
Someday, with you, return.

Bleak these native mountains rise on earth
Long ago as heaven.
Returning I hear your name
By a stranger spoken.
You are remembered among these cold hills.
In silence I keep faith,
Having no title to confess your life
My life, your death my death.

I WENT OUT IN THE NAKED NIGHT

I went out in the naked night
And stood where you had often stood,
And called you where the winter moon
Over Canna harbour rode
Clear of the sheltering wind-bent trees
Above the quivering Pleiades
Where once at anchor rocked your boat.

The mountain isles changeless and still
As memory's insubstantial strand:
May not the living and the dead
Meet where dreaming spirit turns
To the sea-wracked remembered shore,
Revisiting this welcoming door,
Crushed shells beneath your grounding keel?

The moonlit waters of the bay
Move under the December stars
Between the shores of earth and dream.
In the unending Now of night,
In being's one unbroken theme
Your presence and my present meet:
I hold my transient breath to hear
The crunch of shells beneath your feet.

RETURN TO CANNA

Long distances of land and sea
Have brought me once more to the gate
Sheltered by its gale-bent trees,
The escalonia avenue,
As if an old beginning were
With each return rehearsed anew
And I had travelled back through time
Towards the welcome of this house.

And in the drawing-room, where all
Is as it was, or little changed,
As in a dream some small detail
Betrays, and warns us, when we wake
That we in sleep had not returned
In truth to the remembered place,
Only almost this now seems then,
The self I am the self I was.

Or as the pictures on a screen
That make a story seem to run
Continuous, one unbroken theme,
Are images that may be seen
Each a still photograph, so here
The abiding present of the past
So clear, I half expect to see
Again the friend who brought me here.

On that cloudless day in spring
So many stormy years ago
When first I sailed into this bay,
Was all my future course laid down,
Was I already what I am
And all the evil I have done
Enfolded in my happy heart?
I called it love, that seed of harm.

I breathe the air you have breathed,
See the sky you have seen,
Drink the water of the one life,
Am what you have been.

My feet in the ever-moving sea:
The same cold waves
Carried us to this shore.
Time joins us still, and space
And living water.

Once I heard your voice
And now no word:
How are we immortal
On whom silence falls?

If you have ceased
Then I too already of the dead:
We are eternal
Or even now are not.

Gray Atlantic years,
My troubled wake lengthens
Between us distances — oh space,
Full circle too vast
To bring ever home to the past.

Borrowing a phrase of yours
To tell of another
I felt I had been false:
I could not write those words
That linked us together.

Polluted tide,
Desecrated earth destroyed:
Yet one green leaf opens for the heart
The shelter of a great forest.

Ah, no, dear God,
I, who here and now
Of your great world
Must bear the weight,
Time pain and sin,
Would not have not been.

"No old age, only sorrow"
A woman said; all things new
But I. No shadow
The gods cast,
But I my past.

Long, far,
I have sought for the now, the here,
Yet cannot come near:
My every step to the last
Is into the past.

If I choose remorse
Of a heart inured to pain
It is because forgiveness would revive
Joy and love
To suffer all again.

And that was all his life,
His share of days,
Says the grave;
You need not fear he lies
With another,
For him no more
Than the one life I spoiled for him,
And I live on.

I have come too late
To this shore of dream,
To break of waves,
To yellow iris bloom:
Memory has dimmed my sight.

Banked winter cloud,
Clear Northern sky
And the flash of Oighsgear light:
One far star
Poignant as joy
Signals for ever.

Oval the golden moon
Hangs in the evening sky
Filling the bay with light,
So near,
If I could clear my sight,
Cast body away,
I would be here.

Still skies, still seas
So like a memory lie
In mind's eye
It may be you return
Dreaming you sail these isles
To find these isles your dream.

A rainbow, beautiful and clear light,
Whose span, at certain times, a way
Opens, I saw today,
On your far grave its radiant foot.

EIDER AFLOAT IN THE BAY

Eider afloat in the bay,
Cloud-capped isles far out,
This thyme-sweet turf I tread,
Real under my feet,

These were your world,
Your loved and known;
Can you recall to mind
Wrack-strewn shore and tide-wet stone?

I seek you in wave-wrought shell,
In wild bird's eye:
What country have the dead
But memory?

We who travel time
Call past and gone
Remembered days that those who dream
Call home.

IT WAS OUR SOLITUDE WE SHARED

It was our solitude we shared,
Contours of far hills, ferny lynn,
Grain of lichen on wind-worn stone,
Creviced flowers, birds on the wind,
A country where there are no names
For the one being of living things.

It seemed that I had known you long,
That, meeting, we had each come home.
I did not think how all in time
Must hurt and harm, must hate and fear,
But found our parted selves betrayed.

I CALL YOUR NAME

I call your name,
But if you should reply
How shall I know your voice
In sound of wind and wave,
In sea-bird's cry?

Or if from sleep
Some image rise
Though angel-bright, how know
Among the mingling currents of the dreaming deep
It tells of you?

Or does my doubt impede
Those messengers
Whose footsteps everwhere and always come and go,
The world a single thought
Wherein the one love seeks, and in a thousand ways
Answering, the one love replies.

CROSSING THE SOUND I SUMMONED YOU IN THOUGHT

Crossing the sound I summoned you in thought
To look out of my eyes at sea and sky,
Soft clouds sheltering those hills that once you knew
And sea-paths where you sailed,
The white birds following your boat from isle to isle.
Would it have seemed to you still beautiful, this world?
Or from that other state
Do you discern a darkness in our light,
The cloud of blood that veils our skies,
And in the labouring wings of hungry gulls
The weight of death? If it be so,
Dear love, I would not call you back
To bear again the heaviness of earth
Upon the impulse of your joy,
Locked in a living skull your thought,
Your vision shut with human eyes.

KORE

Once more
The yellow iris on the wrack-strewn shore
Blooms in our midsummer
Whose root is in that realm
Where the dead are
Everywhere underfoot
Where the salt of the sea makes sweet the grass of the land.
Among the roots of the turf the fine sea-sand
Of innumerable broken shells
Makes fertile root and flower.
Bright forms return:
Not once, but in multitude is shown
In signature of living gold the mystery
Of immortal joy.

IN MEMORY OF A FRIEND
Bernard Wall, died May 1974

Friend who by requiem
Freed from this world have gone
To be among the dead
Who were your friends and mine
Within our span of time,
How often we have spoken
Of the heart's distances,
The void that lies between
Their state and ours. It seems
Strange that you should be there,
I here, who lately talked
Of these things by your fire,
Drinking Italian wine,
Your Dante in your hand;
Strange we no longer can
Hold converse, as before.

And yet I seem to see
You in the mind's eye
Smile and sign to me,
From nowhere in this sky
Or where the sunlight falls;
But as a mirror's space
Opens before sight
A room no feet can tread,
It may be that you cast
Your presence in my glass
Turn, in that inner room,
Smiling to sign goodbye
From that place where you seem.

We spoke of Dante's dream:
Sweet hue of sapphire morn
In earth's midsummer skies
Seemed metaphor to tell
How clear the light that shone
At dawn across those seas
That ring his mountain isle.
And did you take the book
Of Dante in your hand?
His words can you recall
In that enchanted land
Where all is of the mind
That builds the hells and heavens
And cloudy lands between,
As you believed, and I?

But what's belief, when we,
Closing our eyes in sleep
Believe whatever seems,
And in the dream of death
Must close our eyes on dreams?
And is it we who tread,
Sleep-wandering, strange ways
That lead us to the place
We never find again?
And is it they we meet
Who bear in dream the names
Of some we loved, but wear
An aspect strange and far?
Who knows how they will seem,
Or in what house we'll greet
The friend we parted from
At a familiar door?

To raise the walls of Dis,
The groves of Paradise,
The visions of the dead
Must be less tenuous,
Less shadow-like than ours
Whose bodily senses cloud
Imagination's sight
Or dim its eye with tears.

There was a now and here
That once we called a world
But now a memory,
Where you in time and place
Were present for a space:
Your gentle form is there
For ever in the mind
That knows our then as now,
Knows time's far as near
As thought of friend for friend.

BEFORE THE ACCUSER

The past, the past,
Record I cannot understand,
Though leaf by turning leaf I wrote
That indecipherable script,
Page by laborious page
Inscribed those memories that burn,
Memories that fade,
And memories that seem
Pictures of another life than mine.
Forgotten scenes return, forgotten faces —
What do I know of what has been,
What do I know of those I knew,
Or of the part I played
In lives my life has changed for ill
Or, it may be, for good, since all
Things work the good of those who love,
(For God, it has been said, is love,
A word no less mysterious and strange
Than the unutterable Name.)
Yet I have tried, these many years,
To open that closed book, to read
The sentence of the god within
Who judges all, searched memory
For comfort, and found none,
For all that I have done and been
Was marred by ignorance or passion
Save for certain moments, given,
As it seems, from beyond time, a vision
I had not merited, nor earned,
So great the beauty I have seen.

I try, I try to justify,
To find for ill beginning some good end,
Or hidden wisdom, though not mine,
In idiot's tale, but find instead
A foolish record by a fool scanned.
And in the story there is more pain
Than I can bear to know again,
Yet why it seemed I suffered so
No longer can recall, nor feel
Vanished pain or vanished pleasure.
It is not the passionate cause
But the enacted deed remains
And all its consequence for ever.

A poor story, best forgotten —
But not one moment of the whole
Of the enacted life can fade
From the continuous scroll of time,
Nor is the deed undone by death,
Yeats tells, who studied with the dead:
The soul, plucked naked from its sheath
Knows all it knew, and lives again
All the past present in one burning pain
Unless that life be pure,
And who of all the living shall endure
To be made judge of what has been?
Up and down the track of time I run
Seeking escape in vain,
Take up the Book of Life, write on.

ALL THAT IS

All that is:
The unbroken surface of the sea
Bears ships and isles,
Shell-duck and eider in the bay;
Wings soar, wild voices cry.

Shining waves
Cast up fresh shells
On the sweet turf that covers the fine sand
Of innumerable gleaming lives.
Light fills all space
And all life joy,
All shores the sea: no place
For what has ceased to be.

BLUE BUTTERFLIES' EYED WINGS

Blue butterflies' eyed wings,
Eyed buzzard high in blue sky,
Mountain isles blue veiled
In fleeting shade of fleeting cloud,
Of these I am the I.

SORROW, SORROW

Sorrow, sorrow
Inwoven with these skies, these seas,
Sun's smile and shadow
Over still hills moving mist and cloud,
Gull and gannet in flight, eider at rest on the wave,
Plunge and soaring of life, seabird's lonely cry,
Yellow iris where the seaweed dries
On shell-strewn grass above the tide
And on the thorn the sweet white rose:
My heart no longer knows
An old sorrow from an older joy.

PETAL OF WHITE ROSE

Petal of white rose
And rosy shell
Cast up by the tide:
Who can tell
This burnet sweetness
From memory,
From the deep sea
Record of a life
Shaped by the restless wave.

ON BASALT ORGAN-PIPES

On basalt organ-pipes
The wind tunes harmonies.
Sweet humming voices rise and fall
In murmur of the rocks and the wind's choir.
I overheard them singing
The song few hear
But the buzzard on the crag, the rabbit on the hill.

TURNER'S SEAS

We call them beautiful
Turner's apalling seas, shipwreck and deluge
Where man's contraptions, mast and hull,
Lurch, capsize, shatter to driftwood in the whelming surge and swell,
Men and women like spindrift hurled in spray
And no survivors in those sliding glassy graves.
Doomed seafarers on unfathomed waters,
We yet call beautiful those gleaming gulphs that break in foam,
Beautiful the storm-foreboding skies, the lurid west,
Beautiful the white radiance that dissolves all.
What recognition from what deep source cries
Glory to the universal light that walks the ever-running waves,
What memory deeper than fear, what recollection of untrammelled
                                                    joy
Our scattered falling drops retain of gleaming ocean's unending play?

TIR NA'N OGE

A woman old
I have been so many selves that I am none,
No longer anyone
With a life-story that could lead
To heart's desire, or take away
Anything I would have or hold.
What is gratified desire
To the heart free of hope and fear
That has no wish at all,
Awaits no message but the call
Of birds, the sound of sea and wind?
What embrace or clasp of hand
Brings life to life more near
Than sky to eye, than sea to ear,
Wind on wave and wave on strand?

Sight has no memory,
For ever young
Or aged with the wisdom of all years,
The unbeginning and unending theme
Whose teller and whose tale I am,
No older than each morning's sky
In all the generations winged
Summer by summer on these shores,
Moment by moment all things new:
The immortal hour is always now.

Being that is now, is here
Black-backed gull and yellow iris, sea-wrack in rocky pool
Lifting and falling in the tide, blue space
Where high over basalt crag two buzzards swing
And on wild thyme alight the small blue butterflies,
And distant isles
Whose blue hills float on luminous air:
How could form of wave and leaf and wing
Not please the mind of wing and leaf?
Closer than breath of life
These skies, these seas
On whose waters I am a wave,
Of whose air I am a tune,
Of whose earth I am grass,
Of whose fire I am eyes?

RECORD-PLAYER

Lipatti's fingers, Chopin's phrase —
From silence of what mind
Does melody flow on waves of air
Imparting to the sensitive ear
Knowledge of beatitude
Serving no mortal end or need,
Remote from pleasure as from pain?

Where did they learn immortal joy,
Perfect musicians who died young,
What wisdom guides their fleeting hands
From ivory and from ebony
To strike the dark notes with the bright?
All that recollection brings
From some undying happy state
Refined their fingers to such skill.

Hands that labour, hands that pray,
Hands that comfort and that kill
In life's tasks outworn by toil,
Transient use of flesh and blood,
Strive towards an end unknown:
This beauty is the term of all,
Whose melody attuned the heart
Before Chopin found his key.

THE POET ANSWERS THE ACCUSER

No matter what I am,
For if I tell of winter lightning, stars and hail,
Of white waves, pale Hebridean sun,
It is not I who see, who hear, who tell, but all
Those cloud-born drops the scattering wind has blown
To be regathered in the stream of ocean,
The many in the one;
For these I am,
Water, wind and stone I am,
Gray birds that ride the storm and the cold waves I am,
And what can my words say,
Who am a drop in ocean's spray,
A bubble of white foam,
Who am a breath of wandering air,
But what the elements in me cry
That in my making take their joy,
In my unmaking go their way?
I am, but do not know, my song,
Nor to what scale my sense is tuned
Whose music trembles through me and flows on.
A note struck by the stars I am,
A memory-trace of sun and moon and moving waters,
A voice of the unnumbered dead, fleeting as they —
What matter who I am?

THE ACCUSER ANSWERED

Who knows if saint's or sinner's hand
Carved divine lineaments in stone?
Piano, flute and violin
Respond to bad men as to good,
Chaste Galahad was son
Of Lancelot that adulterer:
In blood, in stone, the fruits alone
Transcend and justify the maker.

WIND

Companionless,
Without trace you are,
Without identity,
Without person or place,
Without name or destination,
Unbeginning, unending, unresting,
Are but speed and motion,
Crying without voice,
Without memory lamenting,
Without grief moaning, without anger storming,
Singing without joy, whistling to no-one:
Signifying nothing wind
You are yet of my kind,
Habitant of the same hills,
Wanderer over the same waters,
Beater against cliff-face,
We are the one world's way,
Move in the universal courses;
You blow over,
Breath through me always.

CLOUD

Never alone
While over unending sky
Clouds move for ever.
Calling them beautiful
Humanity is in love with creatures of mist.
Born on the wind they rest,
Tenuous, without surface,
Passive stream from shape to shape,
Being with being melting breast with cloudy breast.
Ah could we like these
In freedom move in peace on the commotion of the air,
Never to return to what we are.
Made, unmade, remade, at rest in change,
From visible to invisible they pass
Or gather over the desolate hills
Veils of forgetfulness
Or with reflected splendour evening gray
Charged with fiery gold and burning rose,
Their watery shapes shrines of the sun's glory.

WINTER PARADISE

Now I am old and free from time
How spacious life,
Unbeginning unending sky where the wind blows
The ever-moving clouds and clouds of starlings on the wing,
Chaffinch and apple-leaf across my garden lawn,
Winter paradise
With its own birds and daisies
And all the near and far that eye can see,
Each blade of grass signed with the mystery
Across whose face unchanging everchanging pass
Summer and winter, day and night.
Great countenance of the unknown known
You have looked upon me all my days,
More loved than lover's face,
More merciful than the heart, more wise
Than spoken word, unspoken theme
Simple as earth in whom we live and move.

Harvest of learning I have reaped,
Fruits of many a life-time stored,
The false discarded, proven kept,
Knowledge that is its own reward —
    No written page more true
    Than blade of grass and drop of dew.

Striven my partial self to bind
Within tradition great and whole,
Christendom's two thousand years,
Wisdom's universal mind —
    No doctrine heart can heal
    As cloudless sky and lonely hill.

Now I am old my books I close
And forget religion's ties,
Untrammelled the departing soul
Puts out of mind both false and true,
    Distant hills and spacious skies,
    Grass-blade and morning dew.

THE VERY LEAVES OF THE ACACIA-TREE ARE LONDON

The very leaves of the acacia-tree are London;
London tap-water fills out the fuschia buds in the back garden,
Blackbirds pull London worms out of the sour soil,
The woodlice, centipedes, eat London, the wasps even.
London air through stomata of myriad leaves
And million lungs of London breathes.
Chlorophyll and haemoglobin do what life can
To purify, to return this great explosion
To sanity of leaf and wing.
Gradual and gentle the growth of London Pride,
And sparrows are free of all the time in the world:
Less than a window-pane between.

AFTERNOON SUNLIGHT PLAYS

Afternoon sunlight plays
Through trailing leaves I cannot see,
Stirred by a little wind that mixes light and leaf
To filter their quiet pattern on my floor.
Not real, Plato said, the shadowy dancers,
Imponderable,
Somewhere beyond, the light; but I am old,
Content with these shadows of shadows that visit me,
Present unsummoned, gone without stir.

So angels, it may be.

BRIGHT CLOUD

Bright cloud,
Bringer of rain to far fields,
To me, who will not drink that waterfall nor feel
Wet mist on my face,
White gold and rose
Vision of light,
Meaning and beauty immeasurable.
That meaning is not rain, nor that beauty mist.